W9-BNP-216

Usborne

Pirate Maze Book

Illustrated by
Mattia Cerato, Andrea Castellani,
Rémy Tornior, Mark Ruffle
and Laurent Kling

Designed by Claire Thomas
Written by Sam Smith

The mazes at the beginning of the book are easier and they get more challenging as you go through. You'll find solutions to all the mazes on pages 61–64.

Bobbing barrels

Billy's ship has sunk, and the bay is full of lost cargo. Can you guide him between the bobbing barrels and floating food to join his shipmates shouting from the shore?

Monkey mayhem

A mischievous monkey has disappeared into the jungle with the captain's treasure map. Help him find the monkey and pick a path through the undergrowth to snatch the map back.

Serpent survival

Help the shipwrecked pirate slip between the coils of the savage sea snakes and swim to the safety of the desert island.

Cargo clutter

How can "High-seas" Horace hurry through the cluttered cargo hold along a clear route to the stairs, so he's ready for duty on deck?

Sneak through the streets

Guide Pirate Pete through the port's narrow streets to the tavern, without passing any of the prowling navy officers in red coats along the way.

TAVERN

Deck dilemma

Captain Petty's parrot is loose on deck, but his boots have just been polished. Find him a dry path around the swabbing sailors to pick up Polly.

Meandering marsh

Guide Betty and Bob along the winding waters of the marshy river to catch up with their companions in the other boat.

Shipwreck salvage

Direct the diver along clear paths through the sunken ship, collecting all the precious pearls. He mustn't swim through any part of the ship twice, or he risks being lost below the wreck's decks.

Finish

Pirate emporium

This store always stocks the very best cheese. Help the nimble mouse jump and scamper between the gaps in the shelves to feast on the tastiest of treats.

Coastal caves

The sea raiders have unloaded their loot and need to climb to the only empty cave to hide it. Which hill path should they take?

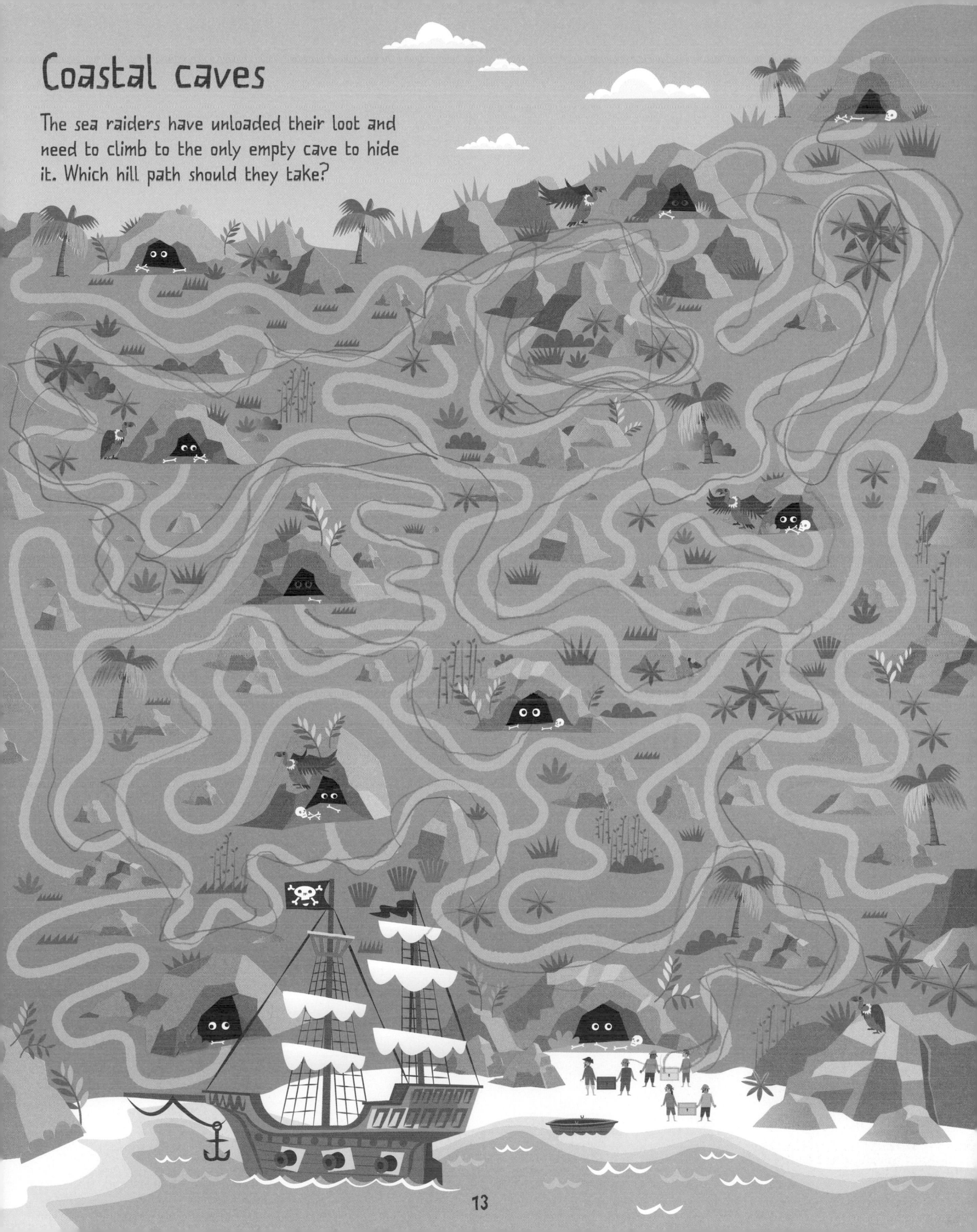

Battle on deck

Find the cabin boy a risk-free route through the battle to the double doors of the captain's quarters, so he can hide there in safety.

Mooring mix-up

Sailor Sam needs to loosen the mooring rope for his identical twin's boat. Which one should he untie?

Plunder party

Claude must carry the casserole to the chef's table without disrupting the party. Can you find him a route around all the decorations and celebrating sailors?

Raiders' refuge

Which path must the pirate take to reach the raiders' refuge at Skull Peak? He can use the ladders and bridges, but he can't jump across any gaps.

Treasure trove

Help the pirates' pet rat return to them between the piles of plunder, collecting the other round ruby on her way.

Message in a bottle

Mog has been marooned on the desert island. Can you guide his bottled message along a convenient current to civilization?

Prison breakout

A band of brigands is trying to release Redbeard from jail. Which way must they go to reach him and escape? They can jump over gaps at staircases, but must not pass any of the guards.

Walk the plank

Help poor Paul take the plunge into the dangerous depths and swim safely to the distant shore through the throng of hungry sea creatures.

Beach betrayal

Ben and Tim have found buried treasure, while their shipmates are sound asleep. Help them sneak past them all along a clear path to the boat.

Ben and Tim

Treasure Island

The two pirate galleons are racing through the treacherous rocks to Treasure Island, seeking its fabled hoards of gold. Which ship will arrive first along the shorter route?

Seabed scoop

Guide Grant's grappling hook down to the lost chest, avoiding the fish, and without getting snagged in any seaweed.

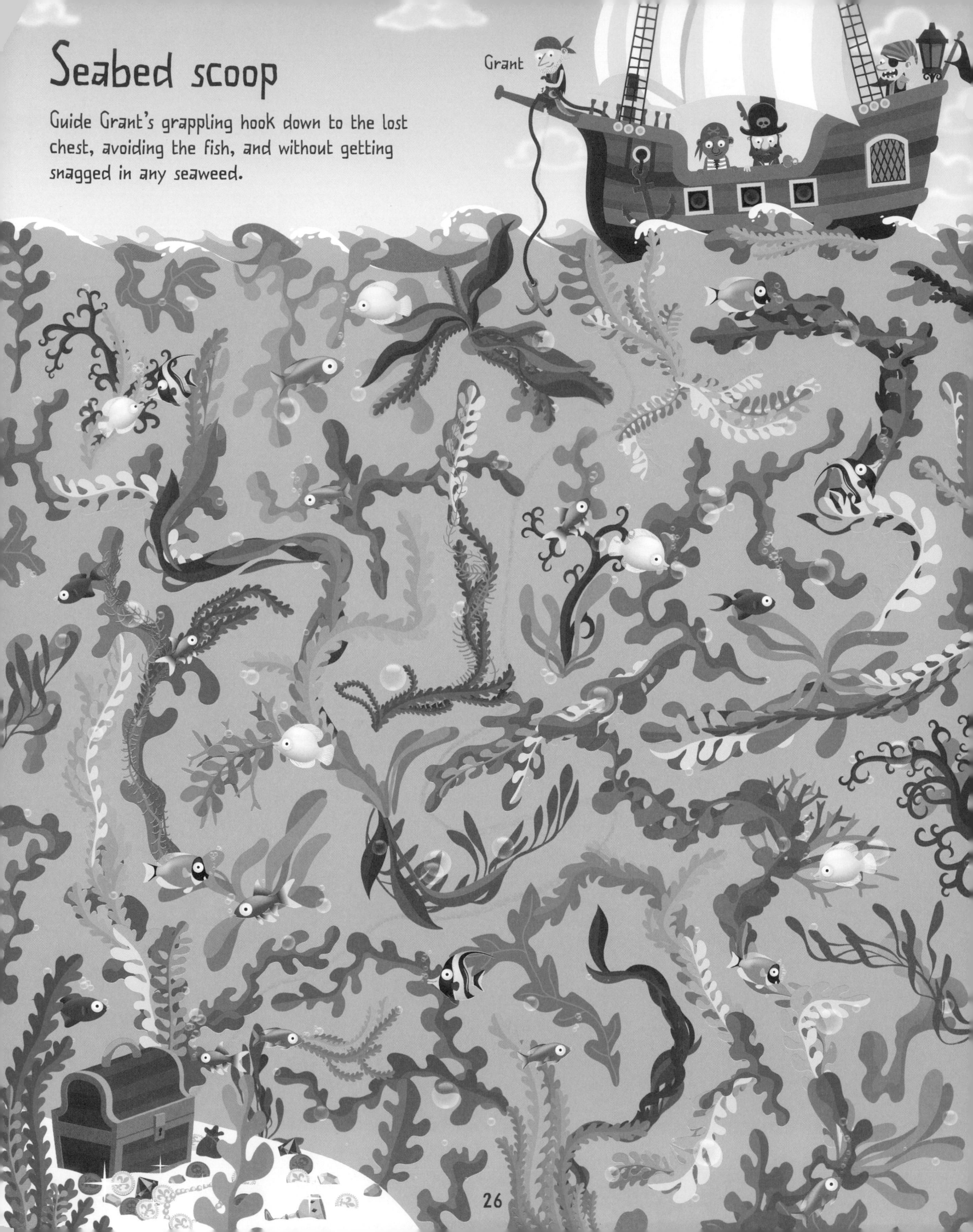

Spirited away

Captain Krill is being held captive on board the ghostly *Dutchman's Revenge*. Map the pirates a route along the sea chart's lines, so they can save him from the sinister ship.

Shipwreck Island

Tom's heard tales of treasure lying lost in the old captain's quarters on Shipwreck Island. Help him find out if they're true, keeping clear of the cracks in the crumbling rock.

Captain's quarters
Tom

Sandy steps

Help Flora follow the footprints to find her treasure, taking no trail twice. The path to the flag where it's buried passes exactly eight palm trees.

Wrecking rocks

The pirates are lost in the thick fog. Guide their boat between the misty wisps, around the rocks and mesmerizing mermaids to the lighthouse.

Secret stash

How can the buccaneers bury their booty below the ancient statues, then return to the ship? They mustn't be seen by the islanders until the loot's safely hidden, or take any path twice.

Ancient statues

Undersea search

Help Colin swim along the seabed, collecting all 15 of the ruby-studded goblets that have spilled from the overturned barrel, without doubling back.

Haunted hollow

Guide Gordon back to his treasure trove, avoiding the skeleton warriors, glowing skulls, bats and any pool that's home to piranha fish.

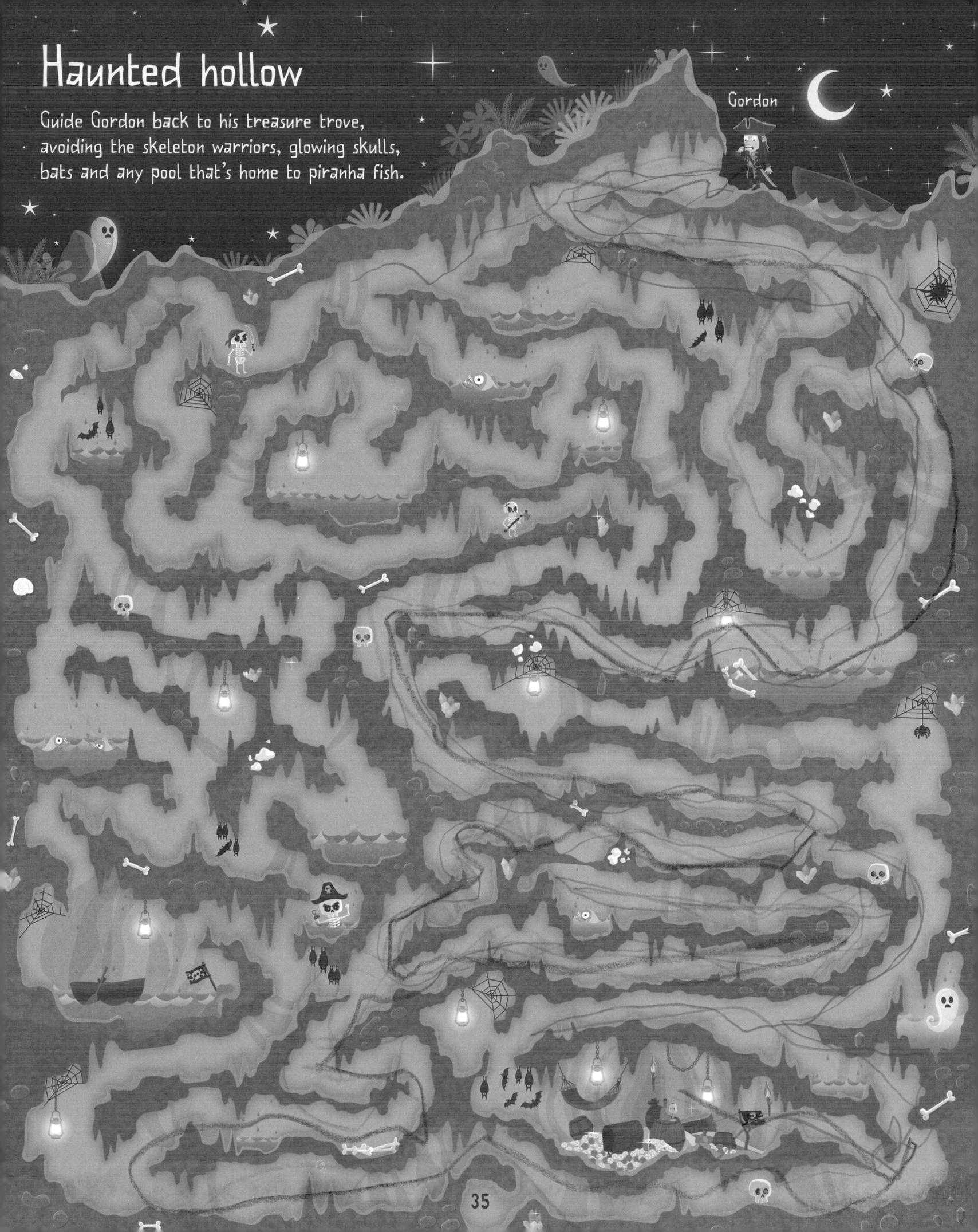

Marine monsters

Which route must Roger row along to slip past the sea monsters' menacing tentacles and reach the ship anchored on the horizon?

Tortuga Tavern

Take Captain Cutlass through every part of the Tortuga Tavern, picking up all the pirates. He's in a hurry, so don't make him retrace his steps or visit any area twice.

Cavern concealment

Help Tilly turn out the lantern in each glowing grotto on her way out to join Joss, so their hideaway stays hidden. Once a lantern's out, it'll be too dark to double back. Which route should she take?

Joss

Swashbuckle swamp

Guide Buccaneer Bill across the boardwalk to the Sailors' Shack, without risking any rope bridges where an alligator lurks below.

Ship supplies

Lead Larry along the streets around the town to pick up the items on the list in order, before rowing back from the beach. The signs show what each store sells, but he can't take any street twice.

1 Pickled onions
2 Herbs and spices
3 Violin bow
4 Bread
5 Mousetraps
6 Telescope
7 Silver polish
8 Boots
9 Tankards
10 Apples
11 Meat
12 Compass
13 Cheese
14 Parrot
15 Hat

Creepy canyon

This brave band of buccaneers believes the stories of great treasure aboard the ghostly galleon. Can you direct them through the Mournful Mountains to where the ship is moored?

Finish

Sleepy scramble

Find Sidney a way to bed, crawling across the hammocks and up and down the ropes. He needs to avoid the rats, broken ropes and badly gnawed hammocks, and mustn't disturb any slumbering shipmates.

Cat calamity

Guide Jack between the boats, sailors and floating debris to rescue his cat, who's stranded aboard the sinking ship.

Island raiders
Help Roland row to the black-sailed ship to pass on the plan of attack. He mustn't go around crossed rocks, or past any islands with people living there.
Crossed rocks look like this.
Roland

Gunpowder plot

In the dead of night, Guy has laid gunpowder on the enemy ship, but some of the powder trails run through puddles, and won't light. Which way must the spark travel to reach the barrels?

Chart challenge

Plan a route for the red-sailed ship to reach the square marked X and mount a surprise attack on its blue-sailed enemy. It must only steer through completely empty grid squares, and can't move diagonally between them.

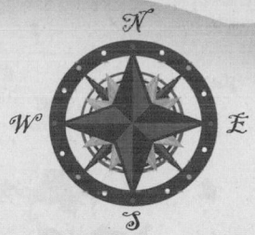

Plate pick-up

How can Carlo the cabin boy collect all the empty plates on the tables and take them to the washing barrels without walking any part of his route twice?

Carlo

Treasure cruise

Plan a route to Golden Bay, stopping at every spot marked with an X to dig for treasure, and without revisiting any stretch of sea.

Jungle jaunt

Find a path for Percy the parrot to fly between the plants and creatures of the dense jungle to join his captain before the ship sets sail.

Pirate apprentice

Pip's been challenged to row to all 27 jetties, finishing with the one by his father's ship. He must eat lunch at Sandy Spit exactly halfway around, but can't use any waterway twice. Which route should he take?

Father's ship
Sandy Spit

Whirling waves

Steer the storm-struck ship between the foamy swirls of each violent vortex to escape to the calmer seas that the lookout has spotted on the horizon.

Lava labyrinth

Vinnie was lured into the fiery caverns by the gleaming gems, but now the lava's rising and he's trapped. Can you help him escape, avoiding the cracks and broken bridges?

Merchant marauders

Pick a path along the trade routes for the *Pelican* to plunder all the other ships, before docking at Dead Man's Drop. It must pass a ship on the same route to plunder it, but can't sail any seaway twice.

N
W
E
S
Pelican

Cannon challenge

Help Lethal Luke load all four cannons, using the cannonballs in his path. He can only carry one at a time, and can't climb over barrels or retrace his steps.

2. Bobbing barrels

3. Monkey mayhem

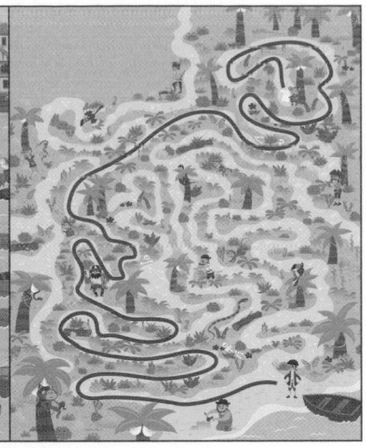

4. Serpent survival

5. Cargo clutter

6-7. Sneak through the streets

8. Deck dilemma

9. Meandering marsh

10-11. Shipwreck salvage

12. Pirate emporium

13. Coastal caves

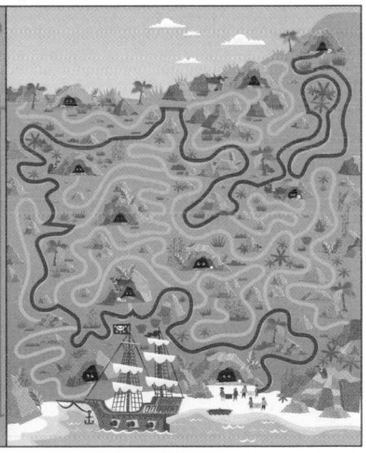

14. Battle on deck

15. Mooring mix-up

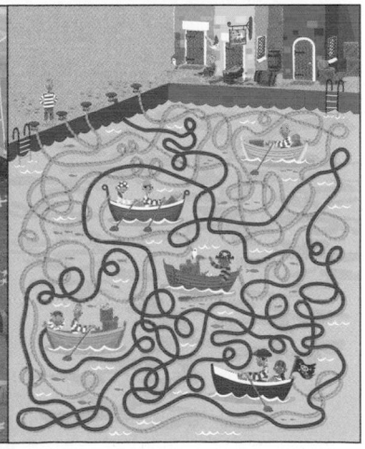

16-17. Plunder party

18. Raiders' refuge

19. Treasure trove

20. Message in a bottle

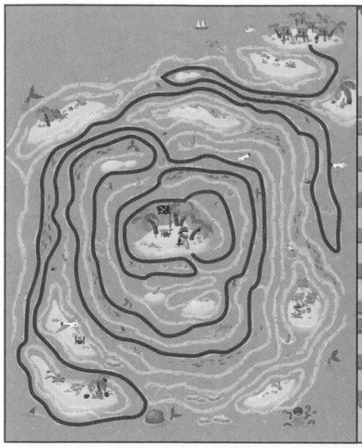

21. Prison breakout

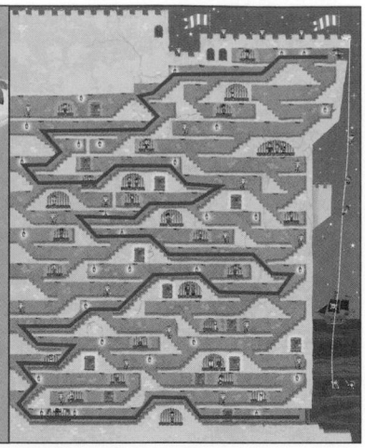

22-23. Walk the plank

24. Beach betrayal

25. Treasure Island

26. Seabed scoop

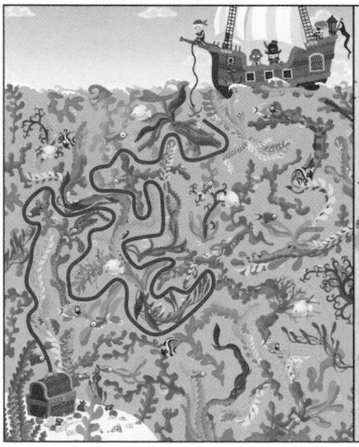

27. Spirited away

28-29. Shipwreck Island

30. Sandy steps

31. Wrecking rocks

32-33. Secret stash

34. Undersea search

35. Haunted hollow

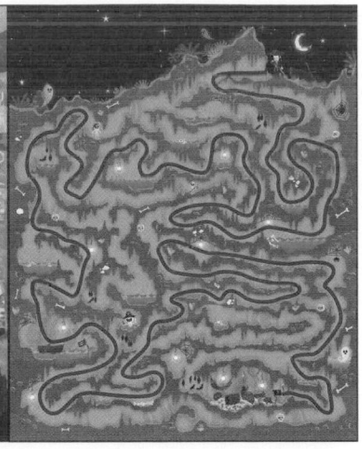

36. Marine monsters

37. Tortuga Tavern

38-39. Cavern concealment

40. Swashbuckle swamp

41. Ship supplies

42-43. Creepy canyon

44. Sleepy scramble

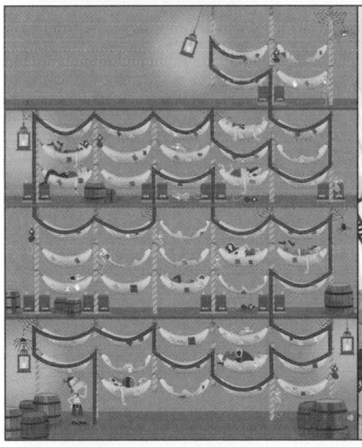

45. Cat calamity

46-47. Island raiders

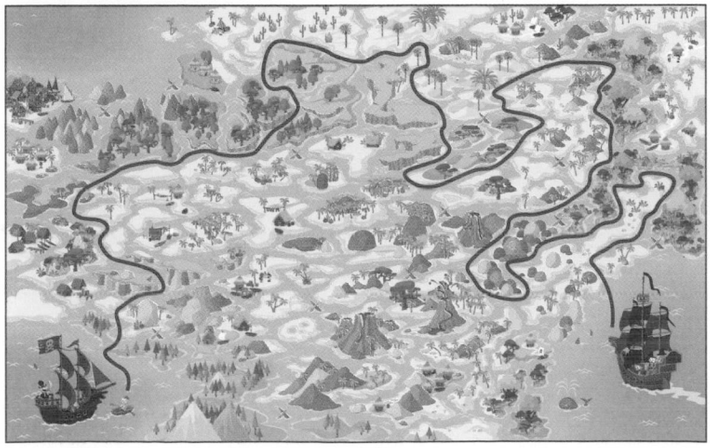

48. Gunpowder plot

49. Chart challenge

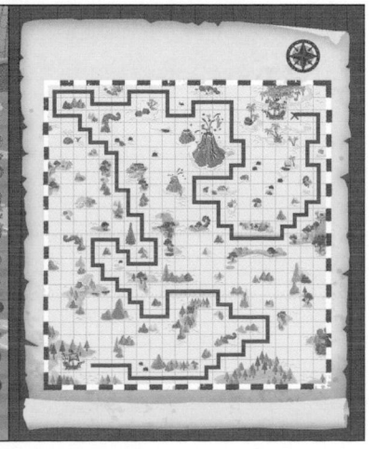

50-51. Plate pick-up

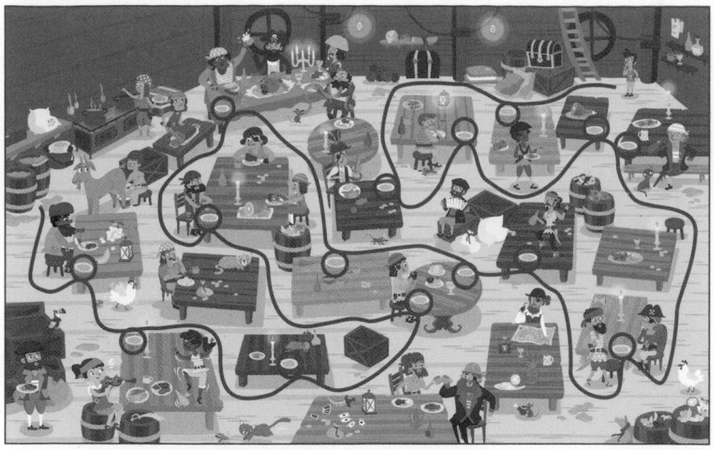

52. Treasure cruise

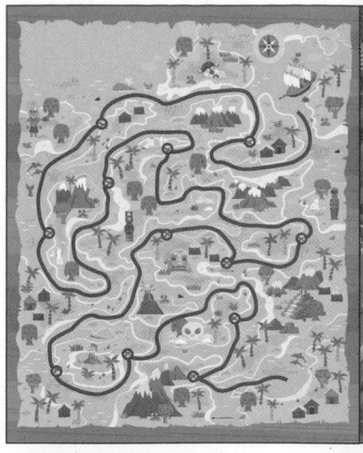

53. Jungle jaunt

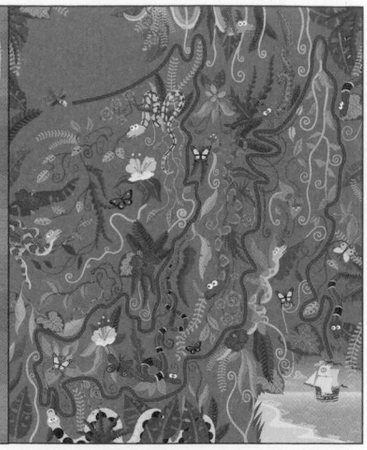

54-55. Pirate apprentice

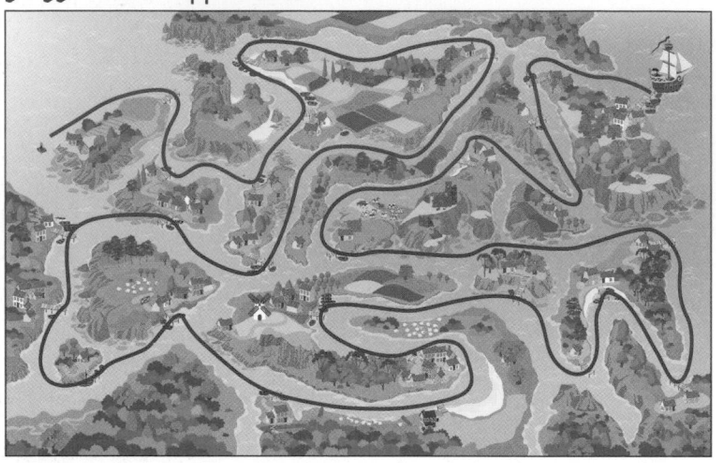

56. Whirling waves

57. Lava labyrinth

58-59. Merchant marauders

60. Cannon challenge

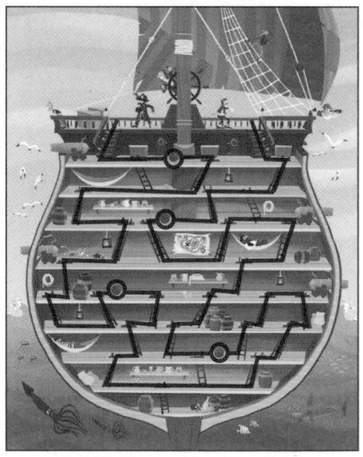

Acknowledgements

Additional designs by Ruth Russell

Cover design by Kate Rimmer

Edited by Kirsteen Robson

First published in 2016 by Usborne Publishing Ltd. 83–85 Saffron Hill, London ECIN 8RT, England. www.usborne.com
Copyright © 2016 Usborne Publishing Ltd. The name Usborne and the devices are Trade Marks of Usborne Publishing Ltd. All rights reserved. No part of this publication may be reproduced, stored in a retrieval system, or transmitted in any form or by any means, electronic, mechanical, photocopying, recording or otherwise, without the prior permission of the publisher.
First published in America in 2016. UE. Printed in China.